Findi
in the Desert

The Art of Drywashing

by Otto Lynch

Printed in Canada

ISBN 13: 978-0-935810-53-0 ISBN 10: 0-935810-53-6

Published by

American Traveler Press
5738 North Central Avenue
Phoenix, Arizona 85012
(800) 521-9221
www.AmericanTravelerPress.com

© 1978, revised 1991, 1993, 2008

2015 printing

Contents

Chapter 1. How to Get Started 1

Chapter 2. Your Trip to the Desert 4
Choosing a Likely Spot. 5
Spot Testing; Working a Gold-Bearing Spot 6
Setting Up for a Trial Run 7

**Chapter 3. Gold in the Rough and
How to Tell If It's Real** 9
Fool's Gold 10

Chapter 4. The Drywasher. 12
How the Drywasher Gets the Gold Out 12
Motorized Drywasher vs Hand-Operated Drywasher. 15
Care and Maintenance of Drywasher 17

Chapter 5. Panning the Gold. 19
How to Pan 20
Practice Panning. 21

Chapter 6. Preserving the Gold 23
Making a Siphoning Tube. 23

About the Author. 25

Other Titles of Interest. 26

Foreword

Gold has always been the most sought after mineral. It is expensive, heavy, and responsible for the condition called gold fever. Much of America was explored and settled due to prospecting and gold mining.

Gold prospecting is a great outdoor hobby. One of the important and interesting methods of obtaining gold in dry deserts is by drywashing. Mr. Otto Lynch's book contains information on procedures for drywashing for gold compiled from over 50 years of productive experience in the field.

The amateur entering the hobby with an interest and desire to learn how to find gold in the desert is usually frustrated by lack of information to assist and guide him. With this book, the author has provided the beginner as well as the experienced prospector with his own personal experiences and professional knowledge. It is written in an easy style as though it were a personal conversation with the author discussing a field he knows and enjoys.

An Introduction

If you have never seen gold as it comes out of the ground in nature, you have yet to experience the thrill of finding a nugget.

How many times have you heard the expression, "Gold is where you find it"? Well, gold might be where you find it, but the big question is—where do you look to find it? A great deal of gold has already been found in the United States and other places— and over the years, people have fought and died for it.

I've never cared about gold for gain or money. The only reason I have looked for gold was the pleasure of finding it. Prospecting for gold is a hobby with me— like baseball is a hobby with some people and dancing is a hobby with others. I think it is the finest recreation in the world to go out to the desert or the hills on a beautiful sunny day, and even though I find only a few little grains of gold here and there at times, and sometimes I don't find any at all, I still have had the pleasure of being outdoors and the challenge of trying to coax a little of that elusive gold out of the ground.

This guidebook will give you the basic information you need to get started and will tell you in a general way what you might expect. There is no substitute for experience or a teacher, and this book does not try to replace the help you can get from an experienced prospector. I can only describe to you how I have found gold on the desert and tell you some shortcuts and helpful hints I've learned over the years through trial and error, which will speed you on your way to finding your first nugget in the desert.

What You Need

The following is a list of equipment you'll need for finding gold and preserving whatever you find:

Drywasher   This is the major item of equipment. The plans to build a drywasher is included in this book.

Gold Pan   I recommend a gravity trap pan.

Other Tools   Pick, shovel, rake, 5-gallon bucket, wash tub, sheet of ¼-inch screen.

For Processing Panned Gold   Magnet that has a 5-pound pickup capacity, small jar with tight-fitting lid, plastic tubing.

Water   In addition to drinking water, bring about 5 gallons (for the panning process).

You should also bring plenty of food and drinking water, a first-aid kit in case of minor injuries and a hat with a brim to protect your head and face from the sun.

Chapter 1

How to Get Started

If you can picture yourself in the desert prospecting for gold, you are probably already an outdoor person and have had experience in backpacking or camping.

Getting started in prospecting as a hobby is not terribly expensive and, after the initial investment, costs nothing in addition to your regular expenses for a trip (food, gas, etc.). You may have much of the necessary equipment on hand already. This will be covered in detail later in this chapter.

One of the first things to do in getting started is to get an idea of where you want to go.

In my opinion, the desert area around Kingman in Mohave County, Arizona, is about the best place in the United States to look for placer gold. It is a large county, very dry, and very rich in minerals.

The deserts of California, New Mexico, and Nevada are also good places to go looking for gold. They are all hot, dry deserts and there is a lot of gold left, though not in such vast quantities as was found in the gold rush days.

The desert is such a large area it would be purely a matter of luck if you happened upon a gold-bearing area, so once you've decided where you're going to go, I recommend you go to the County Courthouse in that area

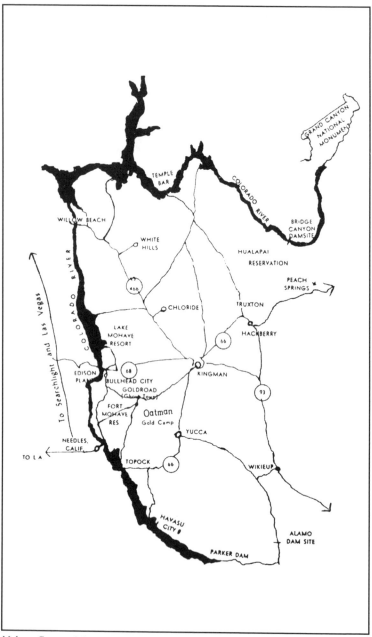

Mohave County, Arizona, is a great place to start looking for gold.

to look at their Topographic Maps published by the U.S. Geological Survey. These maps may also be purchased from map stores. They show the names of the mountain ranges, location of roads and, most importantly, have symbols on them (a crossed pick and shovel) to indicate the locations of gold and mineral deposits. There are lots of placer beds in Arizona.

It is also very helpful to find an old-timer in the town where you go. Talk to him about the best places to find gold. You will generally find someone who is willing to talk freely, give you directions and tell you where he thinks the best place is located. You might even be lucky enough to find someone who will go out with you. If you are that lucky, you will have made the first big step and it will take only two or three weeks for you to learn what you are doing. If you try to go it alone, you may feel discouraged. On the other hand you may be like I was— lucky enough the first time out to find gold. It wasn't much (only a few grains) but it was quite a thrill.

Chapter 2

Your Trip to the Desert

Before venturing out into the desert, make sure your vehicle is in good shape, that your tires and spare are full of air and have good tread, that you don't have an overheating problem (take extra water in case you need it for the radiator), and that you have plenty of fuel.

I have been in the desert for many years and have never been bitten by a snake or stung by a scorpion. Keep in mind that after the sun comes up and it gets hot, most of the desert critters crawl into holes and you seldom see them. They usually come out at night and in the early morning.

CAUTION

There is always an exception to the general rule. Be alert to the possibility of getting too close to a snake or scorpion, and if you are bitten or stung,

SEEK MEDICAL ATTENTION IMMEDIATELY.
DO NOT TRY TO TREAT YOURSELF.

Choosing a Likely Spot

Concentrate your search in the small canyons and washes coming down from the hills. First, note that there are minerals in the hills up above. This is where maps come in handy. Most maps indicate the mineralized hills; for example, the Mohave Mountains, which lie about 4 miles east of Lake Havasu City, Arizona. This range starts near Highway 66 (Interstate 40) about 40 miles west of Kingman. The range is 30 to 35 miles long and goes south to the Bill Williams River.

There are no known rich ledges in these hills, but a lot of small, rich stringers (from the thickness of a cracker to 6 or 8 inches wide). These are called stringers or quartz ledges. Through the process of erosion, the minerals (including gold) are deposited in the washes. Water causes this movement. In the very steep areas, very little gold will be found because the water action is so swift it keeps the gold moving down the hills.

The best place to look for gold is where the hills meet the desert and fan out. The water slows down in this area and the gold drops in the drifts and washes. Up in the higher areas there will be a few little traps found where the coarse gold will have stopped flowing with the water because of its weight. Since the gold is so heavy (heavier than all the other rocks), it settles at the very bottom of the washes, in the caliche bedrock. The sand, clay and rocks will settle on top of the gold, forming a hard pack of sand and gravel. Year after year this erosion process takes place, spreading the gold more and more out into the flat of the desert and deeper into the ground, so the farther away you get from the hills, the deeper you'll have to dig for the gold.

I go out in these washes until I find gold. Most of what I find is granular (like sugar up to the size of a grain of rice or wheat). Occasionally, a nugget about the size of a bean can be found (which weights about ¼ ounce). Depending on where you are, it is possible to find a nugget weighing as much as an ounce. Most of the placer beds in this area were worked years ago, but remember— every year when it rains (and there are lots of cloudbursts here), more gold comes down from the hills. The reason you don't go into the hills to find this gold is because it is scattered over so many billions of tons of dirt that it's like looking for a needle in a haystack. It is much better to let the water bring it together, concentrating it into the washes.

Over the years, with experience, you get to where you can look at a wash and almost tell whether there is any gold there, even though you don't see it.

Spot Testing; Working a Gold-Bearing Spot

With the aid of maps and possibly an old timer to go with you or direct you to a likely spot for finding gold, let's say you decide to start digging there. You test the spot first, since you are here on a hunch and some washes are much richer in gold than others. You run two or three hopperfuls of earth through the drywasher. Then you pan the soil remaining in the riffle board to see if you are getting any "color" (that is, specks of gold). (Instructions on the use of the drywasher and panning are in separate sections of this book.) If you see specks of gold, this is the spot to work. If not, move on to another spot and repeat the testing procedure. Do this until you have found a place where there is gold to be worked out.

Setting Up for a Trial Run

Start with a fork-pronged rake, which is made like a hoe, and rake all the loose rock lying on top of the ground (including all the weeds, sticks etc.) and shovel it to one side. Then using your pick, loosen the top soil and dig down to the hardened caliche. With the fork-pronged rake, work up the caliche, throw the rocks off and get it into small piles. Shovel it into a 5-gallon bucket and pour it slowly over the drywasher screen until the hopper is full. The screen will take the rocks off down to about ½ inch. Run the remainder through the machine, and when the first hopperful is empty, run another hopperful through. Do this three or four times. Then take the riffle board out and dump the contents into the gold pan (instructions on removing the riffle board will come later). Put some water in a tub and pan the material you have just run through the drywasher.

Use a hand rake to loosen the top soil. Pour the soil through a screen into a 5-gallon bucket. This dirt is ready for your drywasher.

Now don't expect to get rich the first time you go out. You'll be lucky if you find a quarter or eighth of an ounce the first day. But when you become experienced in looking for the gold (finding out where it hides), then occasionally you will hit a rich pocket. Then maybe you will take out an ounce in a day. On the other hand, you may only get a few grains. Most of the gold in this desert is granulated (like sugar) rather than in nuggets. Once in a great while you find a nugget.

When you have found a gold-bearing spot to work at, set up camp as near as you can to where you are going to dig.

Have patience. It will take awhile for you to learn where the most likely places are to find gold.

Chapter 3

Gold in the Rough and How to Tell If It's Real

Gold comes in two different forms, termed "placer" and "lode."

Placer gold has been released by erosion (water action and/or wind) and is in gravel and sand. This means it has been placed there mostly by water. The earth has been covered with water six or seven times, completely covered, not all at once, but at different times. When this water covered the western United States, it formed the gullies, washes and canyons coming out of the hills. It also formed what is called a false bedrock. When the earth was under water, the minerals in the water settled to the bottom and formed a crust of what is known as "caliche." The caliche hardened; then after the water subsided and washed away, the action of erosion took place. The rain and wind up in the

Little pieces of gold are still a big find!

9

hills (where small veins of quartz are) caused water to cut through the hills and made canyons and hogbacks, which fanned out into the desert. As the water moved down the hills, it ground the rock and pebbles, washing gold out of the rock. This freed the gold, and because gold is much heavier than anything else, it settled in pockets and drifts. (Gold has a specific gravity of 19.3, while the heaviest rock has a specific gravity of only 10 or 11). **Lode** is gold which is still contained in the rock in which it was originally formed.

Fool's Gold

What about pyrite or fool's gold? How do you tell the difference between either mica or pyrite and gold? A lot of beginners get pretty excited and are fooled by this pretty, shiny (and worthless) stuff.

It takes a lot of time and experience to tell the difference between real gold and fool's gold at a glance. For one thing, gold always looks like a piece of metal; pyrite looks like glass. They are both the same color, but if you look closely, you will see that pyrite is shaped in rectangles or square cubes. It is a crystal. The best way to be sure is to take a piece, put it on a rock and hit it with another rock. If it is pyrite it will crush like a piece of glass. If it is real gold it will just flatten out. You can't break the gold, just flatten it.

One example of fool's gold is the little gold specks often seen in sand, right on the surface of the ground. It would be rare to find the real gold lying on the surface of the ground.

It is not very likely that you will still have pyrites in the remainder of material left after you have finished panning because they are much lighter than gold and will most likely have been panned out by the time you get down to the fine gold.

Another way you can make sure you get rid of all the pyrite is to dry what is left in the pan, which takes just a few minutes in the desert. You put it out on a piece of paper and put it in a warm spot. Then you take a magnet and pick up all the black sand and pyrites. What you may have left then is called sulphite, which also looks like gold but is glassy. A magnet won't pick it up. Take a stone, put it in a metal pan and just run it around the bottom of the pan. It will grind the sulphite so fine it will float right out of the water. Maneuver the pan to where the black sand and other stuff will move and leave the gold all in one little streak at the edge of the pan. Then just touch your forefinger to your tongue and touch the gold. It will be picked up by your finger. Have a little bottle of water in which to put the gold. When you touch your finger to the water, the gold will fall from your finger and drop to the bottom of the bottle. I will tell you some other ways of preserving the gold in the section on panning.

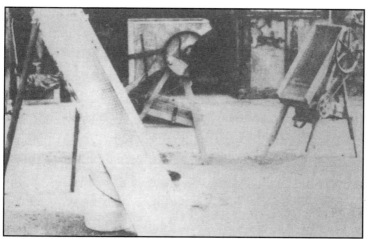

The author used lots of different equipment. The drywasher on the right has a built-in screen. The middle drywasher has a hopper on top. The device on the left is a large screen, separate from his drywashers.

11

CHAPTER 4

The Drywasher

Most gold mining in California (up in the mother lode country) was done by water and sluice box. In the desert, water is not available so you have to use air. Air is almost as good as water. With the drywasher I have designed, I can catch gold which is so fine you can hardly see it with the naked eye.

The drywasher is your major and most essential item of equipment for finding gold in the desert. My drywasher is fairly small and is easily carried (weighs about 25 pounds). It will run 3 to 4 yards of dirt per day.

The drywasher is not really a "washer." Its function is to separate or concentrate the heavy material while sloughing off the light material contained in the soil you are running through the machine.

How the Drywasher Gets the Gold Out

The machine has a frame with a built-in mechanism, including the bellows, crankshaft and crank. The riffle board rests on top of that on a rubber base. Two hold-down clamps on each side hold the riffle board snugly against the rubber base to make it airtight. The bellows box is made so that when the bellows goes down the valve opens and fills the box full of air. When the bellows comes up, the air is blown upward through the cloth (unbleached muslin) on the riffle board. This is what activates the machine. There is a frame on top of the legs with a hopper that you fill with about 2½ cubic

The riffle board, located on the bottom of the drywasher.

feet of soil. On top of that frame is a ½- or ¾-inch screen which slopes toward the ground so that when soil is shoveled or poured onto the screen, the rocks will fall off on the ground and the remainder of the soil and smaller rocks will go into the canvas hopper bag. The end of the canvas bag is a small feed hopper that you can open and close to regulate the flow of the soil over the riffle board.

One of these riffle boards should last for several hundred tons of material passing over them. You shovel the material over the screen on top of the machine. This separates all the larger rocks and lets the screened material go down into the hopper. When the machine hopper is full, open the feed valve that passes the material over the riffle board. Take your hand and pull the stuff all the way down until each one of the riffles are full, then start turning the crank. When you turn the crank the bellows start to pump air up through the unbleached muslin that is on the riffle board. Each of the little pores in the muslin will let air come through the material on the riffle board and will lift the material up and over the riffle. Each time you pump it the light material is lifted. By the time you get to the end of the riffle board all the heavy material is on the muslin down in the bottom of the riffle board. When it gets on the muslin, the agitation from the bellows causes the gold and all the heavy material that is near the weight of gold to slide down against the riffle. Keep in mind that the gold is the heaviest material

you will be running through the machine and will stay on the riffle board as the light material flows off.

Underneath the riffle (bottom side) is a little cleat that extends up past the riffle about ⅛ inch, which creates a dead-air space on top of the cleat that is under the screen. Once the gold gets in that dead-air space it will stay there. The agitation from the bellows doesn't move it anymore. Please note: if the dead-air space is full, this statement no longer holds true. So you have to figure how heavy and how much gold is in the material, and not run too many hoppers over it, because once that riffle gets full of heavy material (black sand and gold) it will start traveling over the next riffle until the fine gold starts running off the end of the riffle board. About 9 hopperfuls is the limit you should run through the drywasher before dumping the riffle board. The best way to operate this is to dump the riffle board once you have run the hopper dry, close the feed valve, and turn the riffle board (which tapers on one end) so you can spill out the rough stuff lying on top of the riffles and pour it back into the machine. Be sure that the feed valve is closed so that it won't get inside the machine while you have the riffle board out. Then if you happen to spill any of the gold back it will still be in the machine and you will get it next time.

The drywasher is made out of hardwood. The reason for the hardwood is it doesn't warp or deteriorate in the weather and it makes a strong machine that will last for years. The frame is built with a crankshaft in one end and two bronze bearings for the crankshaft to travel in. These two bearings are pressed into each end of a short pipe. Then the crankshaft goes through that. That leaves a hollow space between the shaft and the pipe and the ends of the bearings which will hold approximately a tablespoon of light machine oil.

Motorized Drywasher vs Hand-operated Drywasher

There is no difference between the two models of drywasher as far as the resulting gold obtained. It is more convenient to use a motorized machine because you don't have to turn the crank. It is best when two are using the hand-operated machine as one can dig and the other can turn the crank. I use a hand operated drywasher and when I'm out prospecting alone, I dig enough dirt for a hopperful and then run it through. The hopper holds approximately 2½ cubic feet of dirt.

When you first start (when the riffle board is clean) throw a handful of soil on the riffle board, level with the top of the riffles. That seals it and makes the air come through every pore of the muslin. Sometimes, if the soil is fairly coarse sand and you open the hopper to let it start through by itself, it won't even leave the top riffle if it isn't sealed and the air comes out at the point of least resistance.

When you get the hopper full, turn the crank and watch the action over the riffle board so that each time the bellows pump, the material will move down toward the bottom of the riffle. It looks like it is being flowed along by water. Run the whole works, rock and all, right over the screen. The screen takes the heavy rocks off so that you don't run them over the riffle board. When you fill the hopper, start turning the crank so the material runs through the machine. Keep cranking the material through until the hopper is empty and the smaller particles (concentrate) are on the riffle board.

After you have run 5 to 9 hopperfuls through, shut the machine down and take the riffle board out. Dump it over in a bucket and run it through a ¼-inch screen. This will get some more of the rocks out that will be on the riffle board. Some of the rocks will be ¾-inch rock and that's about the largest rock you can run over it. If you get rocks any bigger than that the air is not strong enough to lift them over the riffles. When you dump the riffle board into the pan, run it through a second time, using a screen that is ⅛ inch. (Omit this step if the gold is larger than the screen.) Then you will get about half of the excess out and you won't have to pan it. Take the remainder and pan it and see what you've got. If you want to make time, and you know that you are in gold-bearing placer, what I do is run soil through the dry-washer all day and just dump it in a 5-gallon bucket.

If you turn the crank too fast the dirt runs off too fast and takes some of the gold with it. Just watch it so that each time the bellows pump up you see the material rise up and run over the next riffle. It just looks like water. You run that hopperful through. Just as soon as it runs out of the bag you stop it. Fill it up again. You don't want to turn it long enough to blow a lot of the excess off the riffle board. Leave the riffle board covered. You can learn how fast to turn the crank by watching the action. Make sure to keep the riffles covered at all times so that the material will be about half to three-quarter inch thick at the top of the riffle board. Every time the bellows pump you will see the material rise up and jump over to the next riffle. Keep this up until you have emptied the hopper. Shut it down as soon as the hopper is empty. Don't blow it all off of the riffle board. Fill the bag back up again and repeat the process until you have run 5 to 9 hoppers.

Each time I dump the riffle board, I generally pour it over into my 5-gallon can and when I get the first 9 hoppers finished, I pan that. Before I pan the concentrate, I run it through (depending on the size of the gold in it) a ¼- or ⅛-inch screen. Screen it into the pan and submerge the pan in water. Take your hand and stir it, getting all of the dirty, muddy water and clay out of it until the water is fairly clear. Then you can begin to pan it. Later in this book I will tell you how to operate the pan.

Care and Maintenance of Drywasher

Every day before you go out, use a can of light machine oil to lubricate every moving part. Put 3 or 4 squirts of oil into the hole that's in the small pipe with the two bearings in the ends. Be sure that you don't get any oil on the riffle board, the cloth or the bellows. Turn the machine up on the front legs until you find the oil hole that is in the little pipe. Then put 2 or 3 squirts of oil in it.

Put a couple drops of oil on the crank and each one of the moving parts, which are all metal.

It is important that you don't get any grease or water on the riffle board. If the material is too wet then the riffle board pores will get stopped up with clay and mud. Make sure the material is dry and dusty. The machine must be kept oiled because there is a lot of dust and dirt going in and around the bearings and if you don't oil it every day it will wear out the bearings very quickly. Every month or so, tighten the screws and bolts. The wood shrinks and it will get loose and rickety.

When the machine is not being used it should be kept out of the weather. This machine should last for years if you take care of it. About the only thing you will have to replace will be the two main bearings on the crankshaft. They will operate several hundred hours but when they get loose and start knocking you won't get the full benefit from the action of the bellows. It will cost a nominal amount to replace the bearings. To replace them all you have to do is pull the shaft, take the pipe out, and drive the 2 bearings out. Put 2 new ones in and put it back together. This will only take about 30 minutes. The machine is built so that everything is as handy as possible, easy to get to and easy to keep repaired and oiled.

As you get into looking for gold and working the machine, you will learn just about how fast to turn it. The big wheel with the crank on it that you turn is about a 12-inch wheel working against a 2½-inch pulley down below that turns the bellows. Every time the wheel is turned up at the top, the bellows compresses five or six times, so turn the wheel about one revolution per second. This is just about the right speed.

Chapter 5
Panning the Gold

The first thing you need is a good pan. The pan I use is plastic and has ripples on one side of it. When using a plastic pan you can use a magnet to pick up the black sand out of the pan after it gets panned down to where you have mostly black sand with gold in it. That sand is almost as heavy as the gold, which makes it difficult to separate from the gold. I use a 5-pound magnet (one that will lift 5 pounds).

The author has run the dirt through the drywasher and is now panning the dirt and water, hoping to find gold.

How to Pan

The first thing I do is run my concentrate through the drywasher again, thus concentrating it even further. Then I run it through once more. By the second run, much of the waste has been removed, resulting in a rich concentrate. This concentrate should be run through the drywasher as slowly as possible. If you turn the crank too fast you will blow some of the excess waste off but you are likely to blow some of your fine gold off as well.

The next step preliminary to the actual panning is called screening. Place ¼-inch screen over a container. Screen the concentrate you just ran through the drywasher through this screen. You should now have mostly black sand with very small particles of rock (in addition to the gold, of course).

Now, to do the actual panning. Fill the pan about half full (but not over half as it is easier to handle and quicker at half full). Use a tub for the water and use the 5-gallon bucket to sit on. Rest your elbows on your knees, using your legs for support. Your wrists should be right at your knees.

With the pan about half full of concentrate, the riffles of the pan should be farthest from you. Dip the pan in the water and stir with your fingers, getting the mud and clay out so that you don't contaminate the tub of water too much. Then pour it off on the ground. When this is done, rotate the pan in a circular motion, counter-clockwise (left) as fast as you can, to where the material in the pan will spin around and around but not hard enough to throw it off over the side. After spinning it around 7 or 8 times, and before the material stops moving in the pan, start shaking the pan from side to side and tilting it towards the water. Shake it real fast, quiver the pan and tilt it at the same time until the material almost starts falling out the edge of the pan. Then just dip the pan and pour the water off slowly over the top. It will take about ¼ inch of material off the top (it floats off). Then you spin it again, continuing this until you empty all the grit and rock out of the pan.

The reason you rotate the pan in a counter-clockwise direction is because it is natural for anything to want to turn to the right (clockwise). For example, when you take the plug out of a sink or bathtub, the water always makes a whirlpool to the right as it is draining out. By going in the opposite direction, the heavy material drops to the bottom as the lighter material tries to float, rising to the top. (On the other side of the equator the natural flow of water is counter-clockwise, so you would rotate the pan in a clockwise direction.)

Some people use quicksilver in their pan to catch the fine gold. The quicksilver will pick the gold up and roll it into little balls you can pan out to themselves. The rest of it will be black sand and stuff you do not want anyway, so just throw this stuff away.

You may not want to stay on the desert to go through this panning procedure. When I know I am in gold-bearing soil and want to save time, I take my 5-gallon bucket of concentrate home to pan, where there is plenty of water and shade.

Practice Panning

Before you start panning for gold, practice by taking 12 pieces of #6 lead shot or a dozen steel tacks. Mash them flat. Take some gravel or sand about like you would find on an ordinary trip out on the desert. Screen a

Otto, the author, is picking the gold out of his pan.

bucketful and put it in the drywasher. Then take your 12 pieces of "practice gold," drop them in the drywasher and run the machine just like you would if you were trying to get gold. Then pan your material and see how many of these pieces of "practice gold" you can recover. Keep practicing. When you get to where you can take a hopperful of material, run it through the machine, run it through the screen, pan it and recover all the "practice gold," you are ready to start panning for gold and can feel confident that you won't be losing any.

Chapter 6

Preserving the Gold

When you have panned the excess material out to where all that remains is black sand and gold, take a plastic tub or plastic bag and put it over the magnet. With this plastic shield, your magnet can move material without picking it up. Put about ½ inch of water into the pan and slowly wave the magnet away from the little pile of material in the pan. As you wave the magnet in this manner, you will pull the black sand away from the gold into the other side of the pan. When the black sand has been pulled away from the gold, you then take a siphoning tube and suck the gold out of the pan and into a bottle.

Making a Siphoning Tube

You need a small jar with a good tight-fitting lid. A baby food jar will serve nicely as long as the lid is a screw-on type and fits snug. Drill two holes, one on each side of the lid. You need two pieces of plastic tubing, each about 18 inches long. Force the end of one tube into one of the holes in the lid with the end of the tube extending at least ½ inch inside the jar. The other end of this tube will be in the gold pan. Put the end of the other tube into the other hole in the jar lid (just far enough so it doesn't come out). The other end of this tube is the one you will suck through. The idea behind this method is to create a vacuum in the jar by the sucking action, which is strong enough to pull the gold from the pan (along with the water). The gold will travel through the tube you have placed in the pan and when it reaches the other end of the tube it drops to the bottom of the jar.

When the bottle is about ¾ full of water, unscrew the lid and empty most of the water out, being careful not to let any gold float out with it. If this is not done you will suck water into your mouth.

HAPPY HUNTING

I've told you about all I can on paper. Now you can go out and start putting into practice the procedures you have read about. Practice and experience are the best teachers.

As you gain experience in the technique of operating a drywasher and gold panning, you'll begin to see what gold fever is all about.

Good luck and happy hunting!

About the Author

Otto Lynch was born and raised in Texas. As a boy he had many interests and was an avid reader. He read about gold mining and the California gold rush, which is how his interest in prospecting began. With time that interest became greater and greater. When Otto was 21 his family moved to California and he had his first opportunity to do some gold prospecting.

He bought a gold pan and went to a gravel bar on the Kern River near Bakersfield, California, where, on his first prospecting trip he found some of the gold he had only read about previously. Talk about gold fever—he really had it!

In his younger days, his friends nicknamed him "Rocky." He was a rockhound bar none and made some beautiful jewelry out of agate, tiger's eye, and fire opal.

Other Titles of Interest

Desert Survival Handbook, $8.95

Discover Arizona, $6.95

Experience Jerome, $6.95

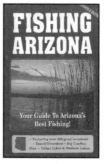

Fishing Arizona, $14.95

Hiking Arizona, $6.95

American Travelers – Gems, Lost Mines, others, $6.95 each

Easy Field Guides – Fossils, Rock Art, others, $1.75 each

To order more books, call **(800) 521-9221**
Better yet, visit **AmericanTravelerPress.com**

Or you can request a catalog by sending a self-addressed, stamped envelope to:
American Traveler Press
5738 North Central Avenue
Phoenix, Arizona 85012-1316